*S*PORTS GREAT

KURT WARNER

FOOTBALL

SPORTS GREAT TROY AIKMAN
0-89490-593-7/ Macnow

SPORTS GREAT JEROME BETTIS
0-89490-872-3/ Majewski

SPORTS GREAT DAUNTE CULPEPPER
0-7660-2037-1/ Bernstein

SPORTS GREAT JOHN ELWAY
0-89490-282-2/ Fox

SPORTS GREAT BRETT FAVRE
0-7660-1000-7/ Savage

SPORTS GREAT BO JACKSON
0-89490-281-4/ Knapp

SPORTS GREAT JIM KELLY
0-89490-670-4/ Harrington

SPORTS GREAT PEYTON MANNING
0-7660-2033-9/ Wilner

SPORTS GREAT DONOVAN MCNABB
0-7660-2114-9/ Steenkamer

SPORTS GREAT JOE MONTANA
0-89490-371-3/ Kavanagh

SPORTS GREAT JERRY RICE
0-89490-419-1/ Dickey

**SPORTS GREAT BARRY SANDERS
REVISED EDITION**
0-7660-1067-8/ Knapp

SPORTS GREAT DEION SANDERS
0-7660-1068-6/ Macnow

SPORTS GREAT EMMITT SMITH
0-7660-1002-3/ Grabowski

SPORTS GREAT HERSCHEL WALKER
0-89490-207-5/ Benagh

SPORTS GREAT KURT WARNER
0-7660-2034-7/ Rekela

For other *Sports Great* titles call:
(800) 398-2504

KURT WARNER

George Rekela

—SPORTS GREAT BOOKS—

Enslow Publishers, Inc.
40 Industrial Road   PO Box 38
Box 398   Aldershot
Berkeley Heights, NJ 07922   Hants GU12 6BP
USA   UK
http://www.enslow.com

jB
WARNER

Library of Congress Cataloging-in-Publication Data

Rekela, George R., 1943-
    Sports great Kurt Warner / George Rekela.
        v. cm.—(Sports great books)
    Summary: A biography of the St. Louis Rams quarterback, Kurt Warner.
    Includes bibliographical references and index.
        Contents: Super Bowl XXXIV—Growing up Iowan—Football at UNI—
        Brenda—Stocking shelves—Barnstorming—NFL at last—Injury strikes.
        ISBN 0-7660-2034-7
        1. Warner, Kurt, 1971—Juvenile literature. 2. Football players—
United States—Biography—Juvenile literature. [1. Warner, Kurt, 1971-
2. Football players.] I. Title. II. Series.
GV939.W36 R45 2003
796.332'092—dc21

                                     2002008393

Printed in the United States of America

10 9 8 7 6 5 4 3 2 1

To Our Readers:
We have done our best to make sure all Internet Addresses in this book were active and
appropriate when we went to press. However, the author and the publisher have no
control over and assume no liability for the material available on those Internet sites or
on other Web sites they may link to. Any comments or suggestions can be sent by
e-mail to comments@enslow.com or to the address on the back cover.

Illustration Credits: Al Messerschmidt/NFL Photos, pp. 25, 30; Al Pereira/
NFL Photos, pp. 9, 11, 38, 52; Allen Kee/NFL Photos, p. 36; James D.
Smith/NFL Photos, pp. 34, 45, 47; Michael Zagaris/NFL Photos, pp. 43, 59;
Paul Jasienski/NFL Photos, p. 15; Vincent Manniello/NFL Photos, p. 20.

Cover Illustration: Peter Brouillet/NFL Photos.

Contents

Chapter 1

Super Bowl XXXIV

His life had been spent preparing for this moment. Kurt Warner had always dreamed of leading his football team to victory in a desperate battle against quality opposition in the most important game of the year.

And now here he was at the Super Bowl, the premier event in American sports, quarterbacking the St. Louis Rams against the Tennessee Titans with the game tied and only two minutes left on the game clock. The day was January 30, 2000. The place was the Georgia Dome in Atlanta.

"A chill ran down my spine," Warner said later. "I thought about where I was and how hard I fought to get here. There had been so many trying moments, so many times I wondered if I'd ever had a chance to tap my athletic potential."

Warner was once a quarterback nobody wanted, a man so unwelcome on football fields that he had to work as a stock boy to feed himself. This remarkable man, who had nearly been ripped apart by adversity, now controlled the fate of the St. Louis Rams in professional football's supreme showcase, the Super Bowl.

"He is a family man and a man of God, an out-of-nowhere sensation whose story has been called too schmaltzy even for Hollywood," wrote Michael Silver in *Sports Illustrated*. "But on the football field, Kurt Warner is the quintessential quarterback, a cocksure leader who wants the ball in his hands when everything is hanging in the balance."

Warner strode from the sidelines across the field and into the Rams huddle. The scoreboard read: St. Louis 16, Tennessee 16. His teammates would note later that he was the calmest player in the huddle. One person who had complete faith in Warner was his coach, Dick Vermeil: "We have an unselfish leader in Kurt. He has an ego, but it's not big. He simply believes in himself."

The team broke huddle, and Warner took the snap and dropped back five steps in the pocket. Tennessee All-Pro 260-pound defensive lineman Javon Kearse was bearing down on Warner with a fierce pass rush. Warner ignored Kearse. He spotted receiver Isaac Bruce along the right sideline and launched a pass.

Warner later told reporters that he had underthrown the ball. At any rate, instead of accelerating as the ball approached, Bruce came to a complete stop. This caused Tennessee defender Denard Walker to drift pass Bruce. The pass settled into Bruce's arms, and the fleet receiver cut back, then outraced the Tennessee defenders to the end zone. Warner had thrown a 73-yard touchdown pass to give his team the lead.

"We were in the huddle saying we've got two minutes to score," Warner recalled. "That's plenty of time. I have a lot of confidence in Isaac Bruce. I knew he could beat Denard Walker."

Observers in the crowd mused that the Rams had scored "too soon." In other words, the Tennessee Titans had plenty of time left in the game to tie the score again.

Warner puts up a deep pass against the Tennessee Titans during Super Bowl XXXIV.

"Then came the longest 114 seconds of football you could ever imagine," Warner recalled. "As much as I love the Rams and what we accomplished, we were battling a bunch of guys who have as much heart and competitive spunk as anyone I've ever played."

With all the efficiency of a well-oiled machine, the Tennessee Titans took the ensuing kickoff and relentlessly marched down the field. The Titans reached the St. Louis

10-yard line, but only six seconds remained on the clock. Then Tennessee quarterback Steve McNair threw a slant pass to wide receiver Kevin Dyson, who caught the ball inside the 5-yard line and headed for the end zone.

Mike Jones, a Rams outside linebacker, flew across the field and tackled Dyson, stopping him at the one-yard line as the gun sounded to end Super Bowl XXXIV. Later, pro-football analysts would call it the greatest Super Bowl game ever played. A tackle on the last play of the game transformed the St. Louis Rams into world champions.

"We showed America what the Super Bowl is all about today," said Rams coach Dick Vermeil.

Almost lost in the celebration was the fact that Warner had set a Super Bowl passing record by throwing for 424 yards. The old record was held by legendary San Francisco 49ers quarterback Joe Montana, who threw for 357 yards in the 1989 Super Bowl.

The Rams dominated play in the first half of the game but had only three field goals to show for their efforts. The halftime score was St. Louis 9, Tennessee 0. The Rams held the Titans to only 89 yards of total offense in the opening half. The second half started slowly, then, midway through the third quarter, Warner hit Torry Holt with a 9-yard touchdown pass, and St. Louis was up by 16. It looked like an easy victory was within reach, but the Titans stormed back on touchdown runs of one and two yards by star running back Eddie George. Momentum was shifting to the Tennessee side of the field after the Rams' Jackie Harris fumbled and the Titans recovered, setting up a 43-yard Al Del Greco field goal to knot the score at 16-16. Then it was Warner time.

"Here it is, I thought," said Warner. "Here's your dream, the way you've always imagined it. The ball in your hands and the chance to lead the winning drive in the biggest game of all."

Kurt Warner runs with the ball during Super Bowl XXXIV on January 30, 2000.

Through the years, many quarterbacks in similar situations have had comparable thoughts. Many failed to deliver. Kurt Warner delivered.

"The biggest things," he said, "are to work hard and continue to dream. No matter how many people told me I couldn't do it, I wasn't going to let go of it. As long as I believed in myself, that was good enough for me."

Warner's story is one of the most inspirational in the long history of professional sports.

"I've had some hard times," Warner said, "but everybody's had some hard times. And all those things have done is strengthen my character and strengthen me as a person, as well as a player. And I don't think I would be the person that I am had I not gone through those experiences. As I look back, everything happened to strengthen me, make me more into the person that I am, and develop my family."

Chapter 2

Growing Up Iowan

Kurtis Eugene Warner was born on June 22, 1971, in Burlington, Iowa. He grew up in Cedar Rapids, Iowa. Cedar Rapids has been described as the typical idyllic Midwestern community, an island in a sea of small farms, rolling hills, and tall corn. To many, it would seem like the model setting for a happy childhood, but Kurt Warner's early life was strewn with obstacles. One of the most disturbing moments in his young life came when his parents, Sue and Gene Warner, divorced when Kurt was only four years old. Kurt and his younger brother Matt were at first confused, then angry.

"It was a tough transition for us," Kurt recalled. "My mother sacrificed a lot to raise my brother and me in a positive manner, and I believe she gave us the best life she could under the circumstances."

Like most kids, Kurt enjoyed watching television. His favorite TV time was Sunday afternoon and the weekly telecasts of National Football League (NFL) games. His favorite team was the Dallas Cowboys. He could not wait to see the team's star quarterback, Roger Staubach, in action. Kurt's Christmas present when he was eleven was a replica Dallas football helmet. He seldom took it off, running about the neighborhood and pretending to be Staubach. He dreamed of a career as an NFL quarterback.

One thing stood in the way of his becoming the next Roger Staubach—his weight. A self-professed "chubby kid," Warner seldom carried the ball in neighborhood pick-up games. "Both of my sons were big boys," recalled Sue Warner. "They could have chosen to walk over me anytime they wanted to, but they didn't do that. We were close."

Kurt and Matt would organize their friends into teams and play football on an open area located in a nearby cemetery. Football was cheap recreation for Warner's neighborhood gang. The only equipment the boys needed was a football. There were no shoulder pads or helmets, no coaches or referees, and few rules. The games consisted of two teams of boys lining up against each other and trying to move the ball across some imaginary goal line.

On occasion, Kurt and Matt were unable to talk the neighborhood boys into playing football with them, so the two brothers played the game in their back yard.

"We used to play one-on-one," Kurt remembered. "I was always the Cowboys, and Matt was always the Chargers. We had some good match-ups and a lot of fun."

In seventh grade, the 140-pound Kurt tried out for football and was assigned the position of tight end. By eighth grade, Kurt was his team's starter at the tight end position. Kurt shifted his dream. He now saw himself someday making the NFL as a tight end.

"He was very much into sports," remembered Cindy Glynn, a middle school teacher. "During recess, he always had a football in his hands."

Kurt's mother was a devout Catholic and raised her boys in the church. On Sundays and special occasions, Kurt served as an altar boy in the family parish.

Warner looks ready to pass against the Carolina Panthers on December 3, 2000.

Kurt's mother enrolled him at Catholic Regis High School in Cedar Rapids. She wanted him to receive a sound Catholic school education, but Kurt was to spend little time studying religion at Regis. He majored in football and, to a lesser extent, basketball at an Iowa school known throughout the state for its athletic prowess.

When Kurt reported for football practice at Regis, he discovered that Coach Jim Padlock was looking for a quarterback. The qualifications were simple—the player who could throw the ball the farthest got the job. Kurt threw the ball nearly 70 yards on the fly and instantly got the quarterback job.

"He was very mature for his age," Padlock said, "and was a little bigger than the other kids. He showed an air of maturity, and the others looked up to him."

Because of his size, Padlock did not hesitate to allow his teammates to take shots at Warner. As Warner recalled:

> Back when I first started playing quarterback, I was one of those guys who as soon as somebody wanted to come and hit me, I wanted to try to run away from them and get out of the pocket. So, the coach developed a drill where I had to drop back and just stand there, waiting until the defensive linemen came in and hit me. I couldn't throw the ball, and I couldn't move. All I could do was stand there. So, the coach developed in me a sense where I kind of became oblivious to the rush. I would just stand in the pocket and stay focused downfield. I hated the drill, but probably it is the one that paid off the most for me.

Football transformed Warner into a leader on and off campus at Regis. However, he accomplished this with a minimum of social activity. He seldom dated, preferring to study playbooks and game films. Yet he was idolized by Regis schoolmates for his leadership on the football field and basketball court. By his junior year, he was the school's starting quarterback.

"Kurtis wasn't afraid to be a leader," said Mike Winkler, a teacher at Regis. "There are a lot of good kids, but many are afraid. They don't want to be 'goody two shoes,' or whatever. But Kurtis wasn't afraid to be the leader."

Leader or not, Kurt still had to spend his summer vacation working to earn his spending money for the rest of the year. He did what most Iowa kids do for spare cash: he detassled corn. For approximately $350 per summer, Kurt and his pals worked in farmers' fields in stifling heat and humidity plucking the tassels off of the tops of cornstalks. They did this over and over until they would reach the end of the cornrow, then they started on the next row.

Hopes ran high for Regis' football fortunes in Kurt's senior season. Plus, there was talk that a few major college coaches were scouting him. During the season, Kurt passed for 12 touchdowns and 1,600 yards. He led the team to seven victories, and was selected to play quarterback in Iowa's annual all-star game. There, he rallied his team to a fourth quarter comeback win and was named the game's offensive Most Valuable Player.

Before the all-star game, Kurt had a sobering experience. A state high school league official addressed members of both squads and told them that statistics showed that less than 2 percent of them would ever make it to an NFL training camp. Kurt Warner, however, was determined to beat the odds.

Chapter 3

Football at UNI

The road to success often is a long and winding one. No one can forecast what toil and turbulence lies ahead. From childhood, Kurt Warner focused on a career in the NFL. He could have never imagined how hard it would be for him to reach that elusive goal.

Along the way, he would have to experience the devastation of swallowing nearly every ounce of pride that he possessed. Impediments appeared immediately after his high school graduation.

The state of Iowa is a college football hotbed. Iowa is the only state in the union to sport teams in both the Big 12 and Big 10 conferences. College football weekends in Iowa can be a combination carnival and block party.

The Iowa Big 10 representative is the University of Iowa, located in Iowa City, on the doorstep of Cedar Rapids. Every Cedar Rapids high school football player dreams of someday playing for the University of Iowa Hawkeyes. Under celebrated coach Hayden Fry, Iowa was riding the crest of a wave that would take the Hawkeyes to 14 bowl games between 1982 and 1997. For unknown reasons, however, Hayden Fry had no interest in Kurt Warner.

That left Iowa State University at Ames, member of the mighty Big 12 Conference, which includes Nebraska, Oklahoma, Texas, and Colorado. Kurt never heard from anyone at Iowa State.

In fact, his only scholarship offer came from the University of Northern Iowa (UNI) Panthers of the lesser-known Division 1-AA Gateway Conference. UNI is located at Cedar Falls (northwest of Cedar Rapids), and its athletic teams play at a level below that of the Big 10 and Big 12 conferences. Accounts of Panther football games seldom reach major city newspapers.

Although the countrified UNI environment has proved to be endearing to thousands of native Iowa students, Warner found himself dissatisfied there. He had looked forward to being Panthers Coach Terry Allen's starting quarterback. Instead, an unhappy Kurt rode the bench. Wanting a chance to play more, he seriously considered transferring to another school. But the reality was that no other college football program anywhere was really interested in a second-string Gateway Conference quarterback. Warner's mother tried to console him by saying that patience builds character. He responded by saying that, by this time, he had accumulated enough of both.

Northern Iowa coach Terry Allen had awarded the job of starting quarterback to a player from Lakeville, Minnesota, named Jay Johnson. Allen was determined to stick with Johnson until the lad's eligibility ran out. Consequently, Warner played backup to Johnson for the next three years. In his junior year at UNI, Warner played in only four games, completing 5 of 18 passes for 69 yards and one interception.

Rick Coleman is a veteran sportscaster with KWWL-TV in Waterloo, Iowa. During Warner's stay at Northern Iowa, Coleman openly questioned Coach Allen's decision to bench Kurt in favor of Johnson:

Kurt Warner takes the snap and goes back to pass during a game in September 2001.

Warner had a lot of ability, but according to some of the UNI coaches, he didn't have the "football savvy" to be the starter. But I would listen to some of the players. Some of them thought Kurt was a much better passer than Jay. When you hear it enough, you sort of try to investigate for yourself. At practices, I would see Kurt, and, in the drills, he would definitely outperform Jay. I would say, "Why isn't Terry starting this guy?" Obviously it would be a risk to bench an upper classman like Jay. Even though Warner was outperforming Jay in practice, the team was winning, and Jay was a decent quarterback.

Coach Allen disagreed with Coleman. "Jay Johnson was ahead of Kurt Warner," he said, "because Jay was a year older, and UNI went to the playoffs three straight times with Jay. It wasn't that there was anything wrong with Kurt. We knew he could throw, but Jay did everything right."

It was to be the start of a pattern that would stall Warner's career for years—he was simply in the wrong place at the wrong time. Kurt was relegated to riding the bench and relaying plays in to Johnson from the sidelines.

"We got along great," Johnson would later recall. "Kurt always was supportive of what I was doing. We studied the game films and helped each other out and had a good working relationship. He was supportive of me the whole way."

Prior to his senior year, Warner's most effective season was when he was a sophomore. He saw enough action to complete 15 of 25 passes (60 percent efficiency) for 273 yards. Even so, what Kurt accomplished in an entire college football season is about equal to what he averages now in a single pro football game as quarterback of the St. Louis Rams.

College athletes who spend three years as the backup to a star player seldom accomplish much more than that in their sports careers. Usually, they are considered to be all-around "good guys" and wind up selling insurance or working as stockbrokers. Warner knew this and was determined to see that a similar fate did not befall him.

At last the 1993 season rolled around. Jay Johnson had graduated. Coach Allen gave the starting job to Warner.

"It was a good situation," Warner recalled. "I was getting a good college education, and now I had the chance to play."

Perhaps it was too good to be true. Warner played poorly in the team's opener against McNeese State, and Northern Iowa lost. Then, against the University of Wyoming in the second game of the season, a Cowboy linebacker went unblocked and hit Warner from behind as he was about to throw a pass. Something popped, and Warner suffered a separation of his throwing shoulder. The injury came at an inopportune time for the Panthers because before he left the action, Warner had thrown for nearly 200 passing yards.

"I missed the second half of that game, but I played in the next one," Warner remembered. "I probably shouldn't have played. I couldn't throw very well. I had a terrible game, probably the worst game of my career that game against Jacksonville State. But we won because our defense was great."

Against Jacksonville State, Warner could complete only 13 of 35 passes. Worse, he threw three interceptions. Coach Allen suggested he rest his shoulder and skip the next game. Warner refused.

"I was going to do whatever I could to get on the field," he recalled. "I wasn't going to miss a game."

The UNI athletic trainers fitted Warner with some special padding to protect his injured shoulder. He was hurting but never told that to the coaching staff.

"From that point on things started rolling," Warner said. "We won eight of our last nine games and finished first in the Gateway Conference, and I was voted the offensive player of the year."

Their only loss in that nine-game stretch was to Western Illinois, when the Panthers were defeated on a last-second field goal. A more gut-wrenching defeat came in the Division I-AA playoffs when Boston University edged the Panthers in overtime after the Panthers' All-American kicker missed 18-yard and 32-yard field goal attempts.

"It was a crushing defeat," said Warner. "and I cried my eyes out in the locker room, knowing I would never play another college game."

Chapter 4

Brenda

Kurt Warner will tell you that he hates country & western music. This may sound odd coming from a man who grew up in Iowa. Country & western music is as common as the tall corn in Iowa, but Kurt Warner did not enjoy it.

At the University of Northern Iowa, friends continually invited him to go and "hang out" at country & western bars in Cedar Falls and nearby Waterloo, but he politely refused. Nightlife was not important to Warner. To him, it stood in the way of football and the pursuit of his dream of becoming a National Football League player. His friends knew this, but they invited him along time after time. Finally, one night, Kurt relented.

Against his better judgement, he rode with some football pals to a local country & western hangout. The car stopped, and Kurt looked around and did not want to get out. Eventually, he wandered into the bar. Instantly, he felt it was a mistake. He did not like the loud and strange music blaring out of the speaker system and was turning to leave. What stopped him in his tracks was the fetching young lady he saw across the dance floor.

Although he would recall later that he had no idea of what he was doing, Warner walked across the floor and asked Brenda Carney for a dance. As the couple moved across the floor, Kurt, after a fashion, managed to avoid embarrassment by imitating the moves made by the other dancers. When the song was over, he quickly asked her to sit and talk.

It turned out that Brenda was a tough, divorced former Marine who was working her way through nursing school. Kurt, on the other hand, was a young, pretty-boy high school football hero on a free-ride scholarship to an institution of higher learning. They seemed to have little in common. Kurt was twenty-one; Brenda was twenty-five. An added wrinkle was the fact that Brenda had two children, daughter Jessie and son Zachary. The latter, she told him, was brain-damaged and partially blind.

"I'll understand if you never want to see me again," she said.

The next day, Kurt showed up at Brenda's door. She was apprehensive about how he would react to seeing the two children, especially Zachary. The boy's disability stemmed from infancy, having been accidentally dropped in the bathtub by his father, who at the time was Brenda's husband.

"Zachary's head," wrote Jill Lieber of the *Christian Reader*, "slammed against the side of the tub, scrambling his brain and rupturing his retinas. The doctors said he probably wouldn't survive, and, if he did, he'd never be able to see, much less walk, talk, or sit up."

After the accident, Brenda sat in a chair next to Zachary's hospital bed. The child experienced repeated grand mal seizures. Brenda prayed to God and asked for a miracle.

"I'd stare out the window," she recalled, "and I'd say, 'These people are rushing to get some place. Don't they know my son is dying?' I never forgot that feeling."

Brenda found God in that hospital room and has been a devout Christian ever since. Still, she feared that Kurt would not understand and would not like Zachary. She did not have to worry. Her fears instantly disappeared when Kurt immediately hit it off with both of her children.

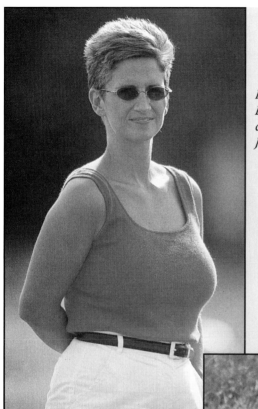

Kurt Warner's wife Brenda looks on during a Rams scrimmage in July 2000.

Kurt and Brenda Warner's young son plays on the side-lines during a Rams scrimmage in July 2000.

"We don't think of Zachary as being disabled," Brenda said later. "He just has to work a lot harder than other kids."

Soon the two were dating, and each of their dates included the two children. Kurt's relationship with Brenda also served to strengthen his faith in God. Warner was raised Catholic and had graduated from a Catholic high school, but never considered himself a religious person until he met Brenda.

His new-found faith and his relationship with Brenda helped to take the sting out of what came next. Warner thought his performance as Gateway Conference Player of the Year would be enough to get him drafted into the NFL. He knew he would not be an early-round draftee but fully expected to be taken in the later rounds.

"Because nobody knew of me going into my senior season, I knew I'd really have to do some great things."

He felt he had. But while winning Gateway Conference Player of the Year may have caused great excitement in central Iowa, it barely registered elsewhere. The first indication that things were not going as expected came in early 1994 when the NFL Scouting Combine chose not to invite Warner in for testing. The tests involve checking the athletic ability, aptitude, intelligence, speed, endurance, and general football prowess of prospective NFL players. Warner learned that twenty-four quarterbacks were invited to the 1994 session. He was not one of them.

Realizing he must somehow gain the attention of NFL scouts, Warner agreed to play in an all-star game at Jackson State University in Jackson, Mississippi.

"This was the most disorganized event in the history of football," said Warner. "We had to take a long walk across an unused field just to get to practice, and nobody seemed to know what was going on once we got there. There were a lot of scouts watching, at least until game day, when they suddenly disappeared. That meant we had to impress the scouts during practice, which was unfortunate, because our practice sessions were a joke. The coaches would hold up play cards and say, 'Okay, let's run these.' None of us really had any idea what the heck was going on, and it showed."

The knowledge that the NFL combine had ignored him did not deter Warner. He felt confident he would be drafted because he knew some scouts had got a good look at him in practice at Jackson. On draft day, Kurt sat by his telephone, waiting for a call. The phone never rang.

But that was only the first day of the draft and involved just the first couple of rounds. Most quality small-college players from schools like UNI get drafted in the later rounds. Warner told Brenda and his mother that he was certain some NFL team would eventually pick him.

Finally the draft ended. No one had chosen Kurt Warner.

Chapter 5

Stocking Shelves

It is well documented that America has an ample supply of former athletes who successfully played high school and college football and thought they were good enough to make it in the NFL. Some still hang around the fringes of the league, while others can be found on street corners and in bars, feeling sorry for themselves. Most eventually give up. Kurt Warner never did.

There are two ancient adages in sports:

1. When the going gets tough, the tough get going.
2. A quitter never wins, and a winner never quits.

Kurt Warner firmly believes in both. And that is why he is successful today. But before he could taste success, there would be many hard times he and Brenda would have to endure.

Iowa winters are long and cold interspersed with an occasional howling blizzard. One Sunday afternoon, Brenda and Kurt were bored and anxious to get out of Brenda's house, so the couple bundled up the two children and placed them in Kurt's GMC truck and headed off for a drive in the country.

"The kids mean everything to me," Warner said. "They are my life."

In the midst of the outing, two problems developed, as Kurt recalled. "The gas gauge hit empty, and we had no money to fill the tank. It was one of those times late in the month when we were trying to stretch our pennies while waiting for a paycheck to come in."

Kurt turned the truck back home, and it looked like they would make it when, as he said:

> The vehicle coughed, wheezed, made a horrible noise, then chugged to an inglorious halt. The kids were in the back, shivering and crying. We scrounged around the vehicle, searching the floors and digging through the glove compartment, and scraped together as much change as we could—about a dollar ninety-five. I grabbed a gas can and hiked toward the nearest filling station while Brenda and the kids froze their tushes off in the car. I'll never forget that walk because I didn't have any gloves with me, so here I was getting snowed on, shivering, with numb hands, rushing back while worrying that the kids were going to catch pneumonia.

Of the two children, Zachary, of course, was the most vulnerable, but somehow he made it through the ordeal without suffering any aftereffects. Zachary became Kurt's inspiration.

"Zachary falls down really hard ten times a day, but he always gets right back up and exudes pure joy. He touches my life so much."

Just when things looked darkest, a telephone call came for Warner from Green Bay, Wisconsin. The Packers, one of the fabled franchises of the NFL, wanted him to come and try out for the team. He jumped at the chance. It was evident from the beginning, however, that Warner would not make the Packer squad. The administration and coaching staff at Green Bay knew this from the start. The Packers already possessed the best quarterback in professional football, one Brett Lorenzo Favre, and no

Kurt Warner, along with his wife and young son, are driven off the field during the Rams training camp in July 2000.

one was going to displace Favre in Green Bay. Kurt was abruptly cut after only three weeks of training. During that time, the Packer coaches allowed him to take only fourteen snaps from center.

"Warner was cut so fast at the Green Bay Packers' training camp that coach Mike Holmgren didn't find out he was gone until two days later," wrote popular sports columnist Rick Reilly in *Sports Illustrated.*

Each year, a sizeable collection of players are invited to NFL training camps across North America. Most of these players have no chance of ever seeing action in regular season games. Yet many return for another training camp in another city the following year, then another, and another, their names eventually dotting the training-camp rosters of numerous NFL teams. When he was among the first group of Packers to be cut, Kurt Warner thought long and hard about his future.

"This was the first time I gave significant thought to admitting that maybe my career wasn't going to involve playing professional football," he said.

Warner went back to Iowa, knowing he somehow had to survive. Kurt, Brenda, and the two children eventually moved into the basement of the home of Jenny and Larry Carney, Brenda's parents. She was still going to nursing school, and Kurt was unemployed. For a while, they lived on food stamps.

For something to do, Kurt would show up each day at the athletic facilities of the University of Northern Iowa to work out. Those who saw him remarked at how forlorn he looked. Just another ex-jock who does not know when to quit, they said. Finally, he took a minimum wage job working for a Midwest grocery store chain, the Hy-Vee. Kurt worked the night shift, so he could continue his daily workouts at UNI. He spent his evenings stacking grocery store shelves, a humbling experience.

"I was making $5.50 an hour at the Hy-Vee store, and I was darn happy to get it," Kurt Warner said. "I'd tell the other guys at the store, 'I'll be playing football again someday,' and they'd look at me like I was some kind of old guy who just couldn't let go."

In reality, he was full of self-doubt but still reluctant to let go of his dream. Each day he waited for another call from the NFL. Friends began to question his sanity. Finally, he received another call from a football team—but it was not an NFL team on the other end of the phone. It was John Gregory of the Iowa Barnstormers, an Arena League football team headquartered in Des Moines, Iowa.

Chapter 6

Barnstorming

There are no major league sports franchises in the entire state of Iowa. None of the small, but plentiful communities that dot the state are large enough to support a major-league sports team. As a result, Iowans are forced to boast of their college sports, minor league baseball teams, and Arena League football.

An Iowa City native, Jim Foster, is credited with having invented arena football. While serving as promotions manager for NFL Properties, Inc., in New York City in 1981, Foster watched an indoor soccer match at Madison Square Garden. Foster reasoned that if soccer can be played indoors, why not football? Foster spent six years organizing the Arena Football League and was the league's founding commissioner. He returned to Iowa in 1994 to establish the Barnstormer franchise in Des Moines.

The Barnstormer nickname comes from the early days of aviation when daring pilots "barnstormed" their planes across Iowa performing death-defying air shows and giving farmers rides in their flying machines. Also, the team's home, the cavernous Veterans Memorial Auditorium, for forty years has been known as the "Barn."

Arena football can be described as a cross between football, pinball, and hockey. Games are played in indoor arenas before raucous crowds. The length of the field of play is only fifty yards (plus eight-yard end zones). Goal posts are half as wide as NFL goal posts and are backed with goal-side "rebound nets" stretched from either side to the sidelines and up to the ceiling. Kickoffs bounced off the nets are in play. Kickoffs are from the goal line at the other end of the field. Sideline barriers signify out-of-bounds areas, and players are frequently "boarded" as in hockey. Eight players make up a side.

This was not football as Kurt Warner knew it. The whirlwind atmosphere of the arena game nearly swept him off his cleats. At first, he thought he could not keep up with the non-stop action. Ninety percent of the plays were pass plays, and teams moved up and down the field like packs of greyhounds. A final score of 70–63 was commonplace. The fact is that many experienced NFL players can not hack it in arena football. The pace is too exhausting.

"We brought him into Des Moines and worked him out," recalled Barnstormers Head Coach John Gregory. "The number one thing he was trying to impress me with was his arm strength, and that was very good. But I also was impressed with him as a person."

Warner worked hard at learning how to play arena football. "I'll never let go of my dreams," he told anyone who would listen.

That he eventually became the first arena leaguer to become a household word is a testament to his willingness to adapt to the style of a game that is seemingly played at speeds approaching 100 miles per hour. And, because he was able to make the transition to the Arena League game, he set himself up for eventual success in the NFL.

"You're under a lot of pressure, playing in a lot of games," he said of the Arena League. "There's that mentality that you have to score every time you touch the football. That caused me to be aggressive."

Kurt Warner is about to launch one of his trademark bombs during a game against the Minnesota Vikings.

Warner threw for 43 touchdowns and 2,980 yards in 1995, his first year in the Arena Football League.

"Kurt was our highest-paid player," said Jim Foster. "He made a little more than $65,000 a year."

Now making a solid salary, Kurt lived in Des Moines during the season. Meanwhile, Brenda's parents moved to Arkansas. On April 14, 1996, Brenda's father Larry Carney was to celebrate his fiftieth birthday. It turned out to be his last day on earth. A tornado struck their home in Mountain View, Arkansas, killing Larry and his wife Jenny instantly.

Brenda had always been known to be in possession of strong religious convictions. Those convictions were now being put to the test. She wondered if God had forsaken her. In her hour of incredible grief, she was supported by Kurt, whose own faith grew stronger in the process. The couple scattered her parents' ashes at her father's favorite fishing hole and, as they did, Brenda told Kurt she wanted to get married. He agreed. It was time.

Meanwhile, Kurt Warner's second year of arena football was going poorly. His passes were being intercepted, and at one home game, the fans booed him unmercifully as Brenda and her children looked on.

"There was a lot of drinking going on in those crowds, and Kurt was struggling," Brenda remembered. "No one knew he had been dealing with a tragedy. I'd say, 'Could you please try to watch the profanity? I have kids here.' Sometimes they'd listen; sometimes they wouldn't. We heard every word in the book."

After Kurt's third season in the Arena Football League, he and Brenda were married in Cedar Falls. Kurt subsequently adopted Brenda's children. Then, from seemingly out of the blue, an official of the Chicago Bears called and asked Kurt to come to Chicago for a tryout. The Bears apparently were impressed by the fact that from 1995 to 1997, Warner had passed for 10,164 yards and 183 touchdowns while leading the Barnstormers to two straight Arena Bowl appearances.

Just when it seemed as if things were turning the corner for the couple, Kurt was bitten by a spider on their honeymoon in Jamaica. The elbow of his throwing arm had swelled to the size of a baseball. The Bears cancelled the tryout and never called back. It was then that Warner figured he was stuck in arena football for the balance of his professional career.

Warner goes back to pass in a game against the Carolina Panthers on December 3, 2000.

Warner had resigned himself to his fate when he received a phone call from Al Lugenbill, the coach of the Amsterdam Admirals of the World Football League (NFL Europe). Earlier in the year, Lugenbill had contacted Warner about filling an opening on his squad, but Kurt had already made a commitment to play for the Barnstormers. In addition, Warner made more money playing in friendly, familiar Des Moines than he would in far-away Europe.

"He had an ability to throw the ball accurately," Lugenbill remembered. "You can't teach that. Quarterbacks either have it or they don't have it, and this young man had it. You could tell he was a great competitor, and it didn't seem that anything bothered him. As the game went on, he was able to roll with the punches and the ebbs and flows of the normal football game."

Warner had an interest in playing in Europe but only if an NFL team would work him out and sign him before allocating him to the World League.

"I didn't know if he [Lugenbill] really understood what we'd been through and where we'd come from," Warner said.

Lugenbill then went about the task of contacting a dozen NFL teams. The first eleven he called turned him down flat. Only the Rams bit. So, in December of 1997, Warner journeyed to St. Louis for a tryout with the Rams. The entire affair went badly. Rams Coach Dick Vermeil did not bother to attend the workout, and offensive coordinator Jerry Rhome said he had other things to do. Nevertheless, it was Kurt's first NFL tryout since the Packers experience in 1994. After it was over, Warner said that he thought his performance at the St. Louis tryout was abysmal, and he told Brenda that nothing would come of it. He prepared himself for another Arena League season. A few days later, Lugenbill called and said St. Louis actually wanted to sign him. Warner packed his bags for Europe.

Warner looks deep downfield in search of an open receiver.

At Amsterdam, Warner came out of training camp as the starting quarterback. "We go into the season opener," said Lugenbill, "and he starts the game. He just lights things up. I liked what I saw that day. The next week he had an excellent game against Scotland, and we won 26–3. The following week, Kurt lights it up again down at Barcelona. We're up by 28 points at halftime, and he's hitting everything."

Warner played in ten NFL Europe games, completing 165 of 326 passes (a 51 percent completion average) for 15 touchdowns and 2,101 yards. He led the league in passing yardage and touchdowns and earned for himself a promotion to third-string quarterback for the St. Louis Rams as the team entered the 1998 season.

Chapter 7

NFL at Last

In 1998 Warner willingly rode the bench in St. Louis, much as he had in the early years at the University of Northern Iowa. He did get into one NFL game, attempting 11 passes and completing 4 of them for 39 yards. Still, when Warner reported to the Rams training camp the following season, he learned that Mike Martz, the new offensive coordinator, had never heard of him. Martz thought he was a tight end. Others in the league thought retired NFL All-Pro running back Curt Warner was making a comeback as a quarterback.

Anonymity did not bother Kurt Warner. He felt he was lucky just to be in the NFL. He had accomplished that much of his dream. He memorized the Rams playbook, hustled through every practice session, and led the sideline cheers during games. Then came Warner's opportunity of a lifetime.

It took a simple twist of fate to put Kurt Warner into the direct glare of the NFL spotlight. The twisting was done to the knee of the St. Louis Rams' starting quarterback Trent Green by members of the San Diego Chargers defensive unit in an NFL preseason game. The injury was to put Green on the shelf for the entire 1999 season and opened the door to football immortality for Kurt Warner.

As one of two backups to Green for the entire 1998 season, Warner was an unknown quantity. When Green went down with an injury, NFL observers expected the Rams to go out and acquire another starting quarterback on the open market. Few thought Warner would be the Rams' selection, even though he had been elevated to the second string in the preseason.

"When Trent Green went down in St. Louis," wrote Nestor Aparicio of the *Sporting News*, "we were trying to figure out whether Kurt Warner was spelled with a 'C' or a 'K' and how he was related to the old running back from Seattle. I think that was one injury that worked out okay in the end. Every injury to one guy is an opportunity for someone else."

When it was announced that Warner was starting St. Louis' next preseason game, few realized that his name was even on the team's depth chart. Fans began to take notice, however, when Warner led the Rams to three scores in the team's first three drives. Kurt felt he was ready to take over the regular-season starting job, but he needed the unqualified support of Rams head coach Dick Vermeil. He got it.

"Kurt Warner," Vermeil told the media, "will play better this year than any of the five quarterbacks who were number one picks in the draft."

Vermeil had seen something in Warner that somehow had escaped the attention of others. Warner, he told anyone willing to listen, is a winner. St. Louis' football fans, on the other hand, thought the old coach was losing his mind. Vermeil had adopted a "sink or swim" policy with Warner, and Kurt knew it. All the years of adversity, pain, and frustration would be for naught if he failed. But Kurt knew he would not fail. He had come too far to blow his big chance. Throughout his high school, college, and professional career, his coaches unanimously testified to Kurt's remarkable arm strength. He could throw tirelessly

50 to 60 passes per game. One question remained—could he consistently throw for accuracy in the NFL?

The Rams' opener in 1999 was at home against the Baltimore Ravens, a young team on the rise in the league.

"This was a huge game for me," Kurt recalled, "because even though I quelled some of the coaches' anxiety with my performance in the preseason, the regular season is a completely different story. The speed and intensity increase immeasurably, and I knew it would be a challenge. Still, I felt confident."

Warner's confidence led him to throw for 3 touchdowns and 316 yards, the eighth-highest total for a Rams quarterback since the team moved to St. Louis in 1995.

"At times against the Ravens, Warner made it look ridiculously easy," wrote sportswriter Jim Thomas. "In the second quarter, he completed 12 of 15 passes for two touchdowns."

The Atlanta Falcons arrived in St. Louis on September 26, 1999, as the defending National Football Conference champions. The Falcons left St. Louis as astonished 35–7 losers to the Rams. St. Louis scored 4 touchdowns on their first four possessions. Warner completed 17 out of 25 passes for 275 yards and 3 touchdowns. He spread the wealth around, as seven Rams receivers caught his passes.

An easy victory over the hapless Cincinnati Bengals was followed by a 42–20 blowout of the once-powerful San Francisco 49ers. By now, Warner had completed 82 passes in four games. Ten of his passes had resulted in touchdowns. The pro football world was starting to notice Warner and the Rams, and the team gained further appreciation after St. Louis went into the Georgia Dome and whipped Atlanta again, this time by the lopsided score of 41 to 13. The Rams won their sixth straight by drubbing Cleveland, 34–3. Warner put the ball up 29 times, and 23 times his receivers caught it. He accumulated 203 passing yards against the Browns. Warner served as an inspiration to his teammates, who knew of his struggles prior to making it in the NFL. They knew he had come up the hard way and respected him for it. The previously easygoing Rams found themselves working harder than ever on the practice field just to keep up with the tireless Warner.

"You have to stretch back awhile to find the best comparison to Warner," wrote sportswriter Scott Fowler. "It's probably Johnny Unitas, who walked off a semi-pro football field where he was making $6.00 a game, into the hearts of Baltimore fans and, eventually, the Pro Football Hall of Fame."

For the first six games of the 1999 season, the Rams had six wins and no defeats, and residents of the city of St. Louis were going crazy.

"In St. Louis, a baseball town, football people can finally raise their heads," wrote John McGuire of the *St. Louis Post-Dispatch*. "They can smile and look you in the face. You know, the Rams were so bad last year that people were leaving tickets under their car windshield wipers. A guy left two tickets under his windshield wiper and came back, and there were seven there!"

But there were still bumps in the road for the Rams. One of them was Adelphia Coliseum in Nashville and the Tennessee Titans. The Titans walked away with a 24–21 win in front of a franchise-record crowd of 66,415 football-mad fans. Warner had proven his arm strength by throwing 46 passes (and completing 29), but it all came down to a missed Jeff Wilkins field goal with seven seconds left. Just when Warner and the Rams got over the loss to the Titans, the team traveled to the Silverdome in Pontiac, Michigan, where the Detroit Lions handed St. Louis its second consecutive loss. Once again, Warner was forced into throwing more than 40 passes, and, once again, the results were similar. When the game ended, the scoreboard read: Detroit 31, St. Louis 27.

Kurt Warner avoids the rush of the San Francisco 49ers on October 10, 1999.

It was up to Warner to right the Rams' ship. The Carolina Panthers were due into the Trans World Dome to face St. Louis, and Warner knew it was a "must-win" situation for the Rams.

"It was important to get things going like we had earlier in the year," he said. "We needed a big victory to get the fans excited again."

Warner started things off with a 22-yard touchdown pass to Isaac Bruce. Then Todd Lyght intercepted a pass and ran it back 57 yards for a touchdown. Warner next hit Roland Williams with a 19-yard scoring pass, and the Rams led Carolina 21 to 10 at halftime. They never surrendered the lead and won easily. Warner's passing yard total for the game was 284. The following week, he threw 40 passes against the San Francisco 49ers in a 23–7 win. The Rams were back on track.

Against arch-rival New Orleans, Warner threw a pair of touchdown passes to Torry Holt as St. Louis blitzed the Saints, 43–12. The 43 points were the second-highest total in a game since the Rams' 1990 season. Week 12 of the NFL season saw St. Louis clinch first place in their division and an automatic playoff berth. The Rams were NFC West champions for the first time since 1985. The victims were the Carolina Panthers, who fell by the score of 34 to 21. Warner was exceptionally hot, completing 21 of 31 passes with 3 touchdown tosses.

Rather than coast into the playoffs, the Rams kept the heat on opponents for the balance of the regular-season schedule. New Orleans fell, 30–14, and St. Louis followed the Saints victory with decisive wins against the New York Giants, Chicago Bears, and Philadelphia Eagles. Warner started all four games, completing an astonishing 75 out of 122 passes. The last two games were so lopsided that he was relieved in the Bears game by substitute quarterback Paul Justin and in the Eagles game by backup Joe Germaine.

Warner looks to pass against the Minnesota Vikings during a playoff game on January 16, 2000.

St. Louis' success in the regular season allowed them a bye in the first round of the playoffs. But it was back to business on January 16, 2000, at the Trans World Dome against the high-flying Minnesota Vikings. The Vikings had been upset by Atlanta in the previous season's NFC championship game and were determined to ride Minnesota's supercharged offense to the Super Bowl. Quarterbacked by pass-happy Jeff George, the Vikings featured the league's top two receivers, Randy Moss and Cris Carter. Minnesota led 17 to 14 at halftime, but the Rams' Tony Horne took the second half's opening kickoff 95 yards for a touchdown. St. Louis never looked back. Warner and the Rams poured it on the Vikings with a lightning-quick aerial show seldom seen in the NFL. Before the bewildered Vikings defenders could catch their breaths, the Rams were on top, 49–17. Warner threw touchdown passes to the unlikely trio of Jeff Robinson, Ryan Tucker, and Roland Williams. Warner and the Rams erupted for a 35-point scoring burst in less than 22 minutes. George was sacked 4 times for 35 yards in losses. The Rams won by a final score of 49–37.

Next up was the NFC championship game in St. Louis against the Tampa Bay Buccaneers. The Rams were one win away from the Super Bowl. The Bucs were known to have the most ferocious defense in the NFL. The Rams came into the game with the most explosive offense. Something had to give. Under Head Coach Tony Dungy, Tampa Bay played a waiting game. His defense would allow a team to gain yardage up to midfield but would then close the door. St. Louis did score twice in the first half, on a safety and Jeff Wilkins' 24-yard field goal, but that amounted to only 5 points, far below the standard set in the Vikings game the previous week. The Buccaneers took the lead, 6–5, in the third quarter on the second of two Martin Gramatica field goals. This was to be a defensive

Warner scrambles outside the pocket during a playoff game against the Minnesota Vikings on January 16, 2000. St. Louis won the game, 49–37.

battle. The Bucs looked like they were going to the Super Bowl until midway in the fourth quarter when Rams rookie Dre Bly came up with a crucial interception and returned the ball to the Tampa Bay 47-yard line. Six plays later, Warner tossed a 30-yard touchdown pass to Ricky Proehl. It was Proehl's first touchdown grab of the year.

"Warner had every reason to fold against the Bucs," wrote Paul Attner in the *Sporting News*. "You could see the frustration mount with each thwarted possession. He was wavering, staggering, ready to fall, as was his team. Yet, who could have asked for a more beautiful winning touchdown pass?"

The Rams won the game by a final score of 11–6. Warner had resurrected himself and the Rams, and St. Louis was going to the Super Bowl.

"As colleges continue to struggle to develop the modern-day NFL quarterback, general managers are turning to alternative, post-graduate sources such as the Arena League and NFL Europe searching for the next Kurt Warner," reported sportswriter Larry Felser.

A 23–16 victory over the Tennessee Titans in Super Bowl XXXIV was the end of a storybook tale for Warner. The winning touchdown, where Isaac Bruce adjusted to the flight of the ball and grabbed Kurt's pass in front of Denard Walker, was the signature moment of the game. It was the second touchdown pass of the game for Warner, who completed 24 of 45 pass attempts for 424 yards. Of his 24 completions, Warner spread them out among nine receivers.

In a special section of the Georgia Dome reserved for players' wives, Brenda Warner saw it all and wept.

"To see a man's dream come true is pretty exciting," Brenda said. "A lot of people have dreams and never get to reach them. To see it happen to somebody who is so worthy, with his character . . . that's so fun to see."

Chapter 8

Injury Strikes

The toughest thing for a major league professional sports team to accomplish is to stay on top of the heap after winning a championship. The St. Louis Rams learned this difficult lesson in the 2000–2001 season. Almost immediately, they lost their Head Coach, Dick Vermeil. Vermeil, who at age sixty-three had been the oldest head coach to win a Super Bowl, announced his retirement just a few days after the dramatic win. Offensive Coordinator Mike Martz was promoted to fill the position.

Despite the loss of Vermeil, the disaster that loomed ahead for the Rams in 2000 was not evident in the early going. The Rams opened the season with a much-publicized *Monday Night Football* game against the Denver Broncos. St. Louis, of course, was the defending Super Bowl champion. But the Broncos had won the Super Bowl in the preceding season. The crowd and a national television audience expected to be treated to the best the NFL had to offer, and Warner, for one, did not let them down. Az-Zahir Hakim took a short Warner pass and went 80 yards for a touchdown to help the Rams to a heart-pounding 41–36 victory over Denver. Warner completed 25 of 35 passes for a remarkable 441 yards in the win.

"When Warner is healthy, the Rams are never out of a game," said sportswriter John Wiebusch. "He is so accurate that he isn't afraid to pass in any situation, and his quick setup and release make blitzing him an iffy proposition. But what really makes Warner special is his knack for spreading the ball around to his teammates."

The Rams' imposing air attack continued its assault the following week when a 41-yard pass from Warner to Torry Holt set up a 27-yard field goal by Jeff Wilkins with 23 seconds remaining in a 37–34 win over Seattle. St. Louis had won, but the defense had failed to hold a mediocre Seattle offense in check. Then, in the season's third game (a win over San Francisco), Warner threw two touchdown passes and two interceptions, giving him six in each category for the year. He was upset with himself and let reporters know about his frustration after the game.

"I hate interceptions," he complained. "but we have three wins in our first three games. I've just got to put those interceptions behind me."

Things got easier against Atlanta. Warner threw 4 touchdown passes, including 2 to Holt for 85 and 80 yards. Amazingly, the Rams went over the 30-point mark for the tenth consecutive game. Sportswriters in the St. Louis area were now calling the Rams the "Greatest Show on Turf." The fifth game of the season saw the fifth win, a blowout of the hapless San Diego Chargers by the score of 57 to 31. Warner completed 24 of 30 passes for 390 yards and 4 touchdowns. Touchdown passes went to Isaac Bruce for 9 yards, Marshall Faulk for 13 yards, Torry Holt for 7 yards, and Bruce again for 12 yards. It was ridiculously easy. The Atlanta Falcons came to visit the following Sunday and wished they had not. St. Louis won its sixth in a row, 45–29.

"Are we blessed to have Kurt? You bet we are," said St. Louis Head Coach Mike Martz. "We have a lot of players doing great things, but we are very, very blessed. You look at Kurt's face when things are going bad, and you'd think we were 50 points ahead. When things are at their absolute worst, he's practically floating."

October 22, 2000, marked a turning point in the fortunes of the high-flying St. Louis Rams. Before a packed house at Arrowhead Stadium, the Chiefs surprised the Rams and won 54 to 34. The key play of the game occurred when the Rams trailed, 27–14. St. Louis had the ball on the Kansas City 8-yard line and looked ready to score when fate dealt a hand. The ball was fumbled on the center snap. The Chiefs recovered. At first no one noticed that Warner was in pain. He had completed 15 of 25 passes up until the botched center snap, and everyone thought he was invincible. But he was not. He had broken the little finger on his throwing hand.

"I'm going to be at home praying to try to get back into action next week," he told reporters. One then produced a medical report indicating Warner would miss at least the next four games. "I'm not going to be out for four weeks," he shot back.

As it turned out, Warner was not out for the projected four weeks—he was out for five.

In their first week without Warner, the Rams hardly seemed to miss him. Trent Green passed for 2 touchdowns in an easy 34–24 win over San Francisco. Optimistic St. Louis fans hoped that Green could take over for Warner in the same manner that Warner had taken over for Green the season before. They were wrong. On November 5, a weak Carolina team came into St. Louis and defeated the Rams, 27–24. The Warner-less Rams rebounded with a win over the New York Giants but stumbled the next week in front of a *Monday Night Football* audience and lost to the Redskins, 33–20. This loss was followed by a 31–24 defeat at the hands of arch-rival New Orleans. These last two losses both came at home, where the Rams previously

Warner burns the opposing defense with another deep pass.

had been unbeatable. A powerless Warner watched from the sidelines, nursing his broken finger. Finally, the team doctors pronounced him fit to play. He would return to action on December 3 against the Carolina Panthers.

It would be nice to report that his return heralded a change in the fortunes of the Rams. Instead, St. Louis played one of the worst games in team history, managing only a field goal in a 16–3 loss. In a word, Warner was awful. He threw 4 interceptions.

"I made some throws I wish I could have back," he admitted. "I'm the one out there playing, and when I throw it to somebody else that's my fault and no one else's fault."

The Rams had lost three in a row. St. Louis had unfortunately followed up six straight wins with five losses in seven games. "I take full [blame] for the Carolina loss," a troubled Warner told reporters in the days preceding the Rams' match with the Minnesota Vikings.

The Rams had handily beaten Minnesota in the playoffs the season before, and Warner had exposed a notoriously poor Viking secondary with long, short, and medium-range passes. Minnesota was no match for the Rams in the playoffs and proved to be equally inept against St. Louis in the regular season. Warner experienced no interceptions, and the Rams easily rolled up 40 points on the Vikings.

"The game plan," Warner said, "was to take what they gave us." As it turned out, the Vikings gave the Rams everything they needed.

The Rams' next contest would later be described as one of the greatest *Monday Night Football* games of all time by NFL observers. Unfortunately for Warner and the Rams, it ended in a defeat for St. Louis. Torry Holt's 72-yard touchdown reception from Warner gave the Rams a 35–31 lead over the Tampa Bay Buccaneers with five minutes left to play. But the Bucs bounced back behind quarterback

Shaun King's 15-yard run and 22-yard pass to Reidel Anthony. The latter set up a 2-yard winning touchdown run by Warrick Dunn. Warner's attempt to rally his troops ended when he threw his third interception of the game. Tampa Bay won 38–35.

In the locker room after the game, Warner was philosophical. "We didn't get it done," he said. "We didn't finish it."

It came down to this: In order to qualify for the playoffs, not only did the Rams have to defeat New Orleans, but the Detroit Lions would also have to lose to lowly Chicago. Warner and the Rams did their part with a 26–21 win, and the Bears upset the Lions. But Warner was not around to see the finish of the Rams' game. He suffered a concussion and missed all but one series in the second half. Before he went down, Warner completed 12 of 17 passes for 133 yards. His 13-yard pass to Marshall Faulk gave St. Louis a lead it never relinquished.

The NFL is full of irony. By defeating the Saints to qualify for the playoffs, the Rams earned the right to meet New Orleans again. Defeating a formidable opponent two games in a row is a difficult task. Add to this the fact that Warner was still suffering from the concussion the Saints had given him the week before. Before the game, he told anyone who would listen that he was fit, but the concussion had resulted in his eyes becoming over-sensitive to light. Little is known about the after-effects of a concussion. All the doctors will tell you is that different individuals react differently.

"I'm not going to worry about one concussion," Warner said.

Warner told everyone he was all right, but he knew he was not. On game day, he was out of sync and so were his teammates. New Orleans raced to a 31–7 lead, helped by three Warner interceptions. The last Saints touchdown came as the result of a Warner fumble. It was a testament to the drive and desire of Kurt Warner that the Rams were able to come back. He threw a 28-yard touchdown pass to Marshall Faulk, then a woozy Warner scored his team's last touchdown of the season on a five-yard run.

"Warner underlies the lessons of perseverance and determination," wrote William C. Rhoden in *The New York Times*. "He reinforces the fading sense that anything is possible, that the American Dream is still alive."

But this time it was too late. Time ran out and the Saints won, 31–28. There would be no Super Bowl appearance this season for the Rams.

The Warners had purchased a four-bedroom house in a St. Louis suburb. They spent the Rams' off-season donating their time and money to the non-denominational St. Louis Family Church and Camp Barnabas, a Christian retreat for needy and disabled children in Purdy, Missouri. Kurt's generosity resulted in more than $200,000 for Camp Barnabas to expand its services and include more children in future camps. His support included donating all of the proceeds from his special Warner's Crunchtime cereal to the camp as well as the fees he gathered for appearances on "Wheel of Fortune" and other television shows. In April, he announced that he was establishing a private charitable foundation. The Kurt Warner Foundation has the slogan "First Things First."

"The idea Kurt has is to create programs entirely influenced by his ideas and goals versus just lending his support to programs that are already out there," said Rob Lefco, Warner's agent. "Brenda will be involved, and they want their kids to learn from it as well."

"I guess it's sort of a storybook ending," Warner said. "When you think about where I was and where I am now, it seems pretty incredible."

But Kurt's story did not end with the loss to New Orleans in the final game of the 2000 season. The next season would witness a dramatic return to glory for the St. Louis Rams.

The 2001 season for the Rams started off with a 20–17 win over the Philadelphia Eagles on September 9. Over the off-season, the Rams had completely overhauled their defense and featured eight new starters on opening day. The new St. Louis defense held the Eagles in check, and Warner passed for 308 yards and a touchdown. The following week, the Rams traveled to San Francisco to face the improved 49ers. St. Louis came away with a 30–26 win as Warner passed for 3 touchdowns. Next, Warner caught the Miami Dolphins' defensive secondary napping and threw 4 touchdown passes in an easy 42–10 win in St. Louis. The Rams won their fourth in a row by demolishing Detroit, 35–0, at the Pontiac Silverdome. Warner threw 3 touchdown passes to give him a total of 11 for the year.

Against the New York Giants the next week in St. Louis, the crowd went silent when All-Pro running back Marshall Faulk, who had fumbled twice in the game, left with a knee injury. Warner, however, led the Rams from a 14–9 deficit to a narrow 15–14 win. The Rams had five wins and no defeats. The New York Jets were the next to fall to St. Louis as Trung Canidate replaced Faulk at running back and ran for 195 yards on 23 carries. Warner hardly broke a sweat in leading St. Louis to a 34–14 victory.

All good things must come to an end, and, for the Rams, the conclusion of their winning streak came in a game against the pesky New Orleans Saints. Warner had a terrible day, throwing 4 interceptions. The Saints rallied from an 18-point halftime deficit to upset the previously unbeaten Rams on October 28 by the score of 34–31.

Fortunately for St. Louis, the next game was at home against the hapless Carolina Panthers, who put up little resistance and lost to the Rams by 34 points. The team then journeyed to Foxboro, Massachusetts, to face the New England Patriots. Warner, who had been limited in practice because of a sore thumb, completed an extraordinary 30 of 42 passes for 401 yards and 3 touchdowns. Another Rams nemesis, the Tampa Bay Bucs, came to St. Louis on November 26. The Bucs capitalized on 5 St. Louis turnovers for a 24–17 win over the Rams.

But a 27–14 win over the 49ers vaulted the Rams to the top of the National Football Conference. One of the most unusual plays in the history of the NFL, a throwback to 1940s college football, took place in the game. As Michael Silver of *Sports Illustrated* described it, "Warner stepped out from under center, disgustedly unbuckled his chin strap and started back toward the referee acting as if he was going to call a timeout. It was the worst overacting, but the diversion worked. Marshall Faulk took a direct snap and ran four yards for the first down. On the next play, Faulk staked the Rams to a 7–0 lead with a six-yard scoring run."

The Greatest Show on Turf was rolling again. The Rams clinched a playoff spot with a 34-21 thumping of New Orleans in the Superdome on Monday night. Warner flawlessly threw for 338 yards and 4 touchdowns, three of them to Isaac Bruce. The Ram's next victim was Carolina in Charlotte. With the win St. Louis moved to eight wins and no defeats on the road, an incredible feat in the NFL.

"We're not going to hang our hat on the fact that we won eight on the road," Warner told reporters. "We want to make sure that we win at least one more on the road."

He was referring to the 2002 Super Bowl, which would be played in New Orleans. The following week, the Rams easily clinched the NFC West crown by blasting Indianapolis, 42–17, as Warner was successful on 23 of 30 pass attempts.

On January 6, 2002, St. Louis locked up home-field advantage in the ensuing playoffs by blitzing Atlanta 31 to 13. Warner wound up with 4,830 passing yards, the most since Dan Marino passed for 5,084 yards in 1984. He was voted the Most Valuable Player in the NFL.

"When I'm out there," Warner said, "I don't think. I just play. Nothing I've done has surprised me because it's all in the realm of my ability. To think that a year from now, two years from now, I won't be able to do it? That's crazy. I will be the same player. I think I can play this way for ten years."

Warner has indicated, however, that he will continue to keep things in proper perspective. "When I first started dating my wife," he said, "she was on food stamps. Then I was stocking groceries for $5.50 an hour. We had to make a lot of tough decisions, and we went through tough times to really figure out what was important. I don't think of my story as a Hollywood story. It's just my life. What else can I say? It's been tremendous, and I am truly blessed."

The NFL playoffs began for the St. Louis Rams with a matchup against the Green Bay Packers. The Packers had earned the right to play the Rams by defeating San Francisco in the first round of the playoffs, 25–15. Experts anticipated a close game with Green Bay and were not surprised when the first quarter ended in a 7–7 deadlock. From there, Warner took over. He hit Torry Holt and James Hodgins with touchdown passes, and the rout was on. The only sour note was that after completing a 4-yard pass to Marshall Faulk, Warner was given a bone-crunching hit by Green Bay's Vonnie Holliday, resulting in badly bruised ribs. X-rays showed no broken bones, however. St. Louis went on to trounce the Packers 45–17, and once again, the Super Bowl was within reach. Only the Philadelphia Eagles stood in the way.

While the Rams were romping over Green Bay, Philadelphia was having a similarly easy time disposing of

Kurt Warner looks to pass against the New England Patriots during Super Bowl XXXVI on February 3, 2002.

the Chicago Bears. The stage was set for the NFC Championship Game pitting the Eagles of the Eastern Division against St. Louis of the West. At first, the Rams did not benefit from their home-field advantage, as Philadelphia took a 17–13 halftime lead. Then Warner and Marshall Faulk ignited a previously sputtering offense. Faulk rushed for a career-high 159 yards and scored 2 touchdowns. Despite his bruised ribs, Warner completed 22 of 33 passes for 212 yards, including a touchdown pass to Isaac Bruce. St. Louis won the game going away, 29–24.

The Rams were huge favorites to win Super Bowl XXXVI in New Orleans. The New England Patriots were AFC champions, but did not seem to have the firepower of Warner and the Greatest Show on Turf. St. Louis was a two-touchdown favorite, but when the dust settled, the scoreboard read: New England 20, St. Louis 17. A 48-yard field goal by the Patriots' Adam Vinateri had won it for New England. Warner had completed 28 passes for the Rams including a 26-yarder to Ricky Proehl that, combined with the extra point, tied the score at 17 late in the game. In the end, however, the St. Louis defense was unable to stop New England quarterback Tom Brady. Brady engineered a 53-yard, nine-play drive to set up Vinateri's winning field goal in the final seconds.

What had been a glorious season for the Rams ended in defeat in the NFL's most important game. It was Warner's second Super Bowl. He vowed it would not be his last.

Career Statistics

Pre-NFL

Years	Team	Games	Att	Comp	Pct	Yds	Td	Int
1989–93	University of Northern Iowa	27	352	201	57.1	3,230	19	16
1995–97	Iowa Barnstormers (Arena Football)	40	1,320	818	62.0	10,164	183	42
1998	Amsterdam Admirals (NFL Europe)	10	326	165	51.0	2,101	15	5

NFL

Years	Team	Games	Att	Comp	Pct	Yds	Td	Int
1998	St. Louis	1	11	4	36.4	39	0	0
1999	St. Louis	16	499	325	65.1	4,353	41	13
2000	St. Louis	11	347	235	67.7	3,429	21	18
2001	St. Louis	16	546	375	68.7	4,830	36	22
Totals		44	1,403	939	66.9	12,651	98	53

Att = Attempts   **Yds** = Yards
Comp = Completions   **Td** = Touchdowns
Pct = Completion Percentage   **Int** = Interceptions

Where to Write
Kurt Warner

Mr. Kurt Warner
c/o The St. Louis Rams
Trans World Dome
701 Convention Plaza
St. Louis, MO 63101

On the Internet at:

http://www.stlouisrams.com
http://www.nfl.com
http://www.kurtwarner.org

Index